"Our time has come! From slave ship to the championship ... from the outhouse to the courthouse to the statehouse to the White House! Our time has come.... Hands that once picked cotton can now pick presidents. Our time has come!"

— JESSE JACKSON

JESSE JACKSON

BY JAMES MEADOWS

The Child's World®

GRAPHIC DESIGN
Robert E. Bonaker / Graphic Design & Consulting Co.

PROJECT COORDINATOR
James R. Rothaus / James R. Rothaus & Associates

EDITORIAL DIRECTION
Elizabeth Sirimarco Budd

COVER PHOTO
Portrait of Jesse Jackson
©Shelley Gazin/CORBIS

Library of Congress Cataloging-in-Publication Data
Meadows, James, 1969–
Jesse Jackson / by James Meadows.
p. cm.
Includes index.
Summary: Discusses the life of Jesse Jackson, including
his involvement in the civil rights movement, his
presidential campaigns, and his role as freelance
diplomat and world humanitarian.
ISBN 1-56766-742-2 (acid-free paper)

1. Jackson, Jesse, 1941– — Juvenile literature. 2. Afro-
Americans — Biography — Juvenile literature. 3. Civil
rights workers — United States — Biography — Juvenile
literature. 4. Presidential candidates — United States —
Biography — Juvenile literature. [1. Jackson, Jesse, 1941–
2. Civil rights workers. 3. Afro Americans — Biography.]
I. Title

E185.97.J25 M43 2000
973.927'092 — dc21   00-027575
[B]

Contents

Facing History

In 1984, a tall African American man named Jesse Jackson walked on stage at the National **Convention** of the Democratic **political party**. He walked with confidence to the microphone, and stood in front of thousands of people. Millions of other people watched him on their televisions.

When he spoke, many of his words rhymed. His speech had a powerful rhythm. He spoke for almost an hour. He spoke about people of all races and backgrounds working together to unite America: "Our flag is red, white and blue, but our nation is a rainbow — red, yellow, brown, black and white — and we're all precious in God's sight." He spoke about the needs of poor people in America. He told people what they could do to help.

As he spoke, the crowd stopped him with their cheers. More than 50 times, Jesse stopped speaking while they shouted and clapped. After he spoke, men and women had tears in their eyes. They knew they were watching an important moment in American history.

Jesse Jackson was running for president of the United States. He was not the first African American to run for president. A few people had tried before. But he was the first serious African American **candidate.** Jesse was not just running for president. For the first time, an African American was running to win!

Many Americans could not imagine electing an African American president in 1984. Most U.S. citizens supported equal voting rights for African Americans. But the thought of a black president was too much for many of them. When Jesse spoke to the nation that night in 1984, he challenged people. He challenged them to think about their **prejudices.** He challenged African Americans to have confidence and to dream big.

©Jacques M. Chenet/CORBIS

IN 1984, JESSE JACKSON BECAME THE COUNTRY'S FIRST SERIOUS
AFRICAN AMERICAN PRESIDENTIAL CANDIDATE. HIS POWERFUL
WORDS AND IDEAS GAINED THE SUPPORT OF MANY AMERICANS.

Image credit: ©Peter Turnley/CORBIS

A REPRESENTATIVE AT THE CONVENTION
SHOWS HER ENTHUSIASTIC SUPPORT FOR
JACKSON. HIS CHALLENGE TO "KEEP
HOPE ALIVE!" THRILLED THE CROWD.

Jesse Jackson was not like other presidential candidates. Most people who run for president are wealthy. Most candidates have had careers in **politics** or in the military before they run for president. Jesse Jackson grew up poor. He rose to the top of American politics without running for other offices. And he never served in the military.

Jesse Jackson was an **activist** before he ran for president. He led **demonstrations** and made speeches for **justice** and equal rights. He fought to gain better treatment for Americans who were not treated fairly. When he stood before the crowd that night at the Democratic Convention, many people knew that American politics would never be the same.

©Jaques M. Chenet/CORBIS

JACKSON GAINED THE ATTENTION OF MILLIONS OF AMERICANS, INCLUDING FORMER PRESIDENT JIMMY CARTER, WHEN HE SPOKE AT THE DEMOCRATIC CONVENTION.

Difficult Beginnings

When Jesse was born, his mother named him Jesse Burns. She named him Jesse in honor of his grandfather, Jesse Robinson. Mr. Robinson was a minister, just as young Jesse would be one day. Burns was his mother's last name. Jesse took her name because she was not married to Jesse's father. Jesse's mother was named Helen Burns. She was just a teenager when he was born.

Jesse's birth upset many African Americans in Greenville, South Carolina. In 1941, many people thought it was shameful to have a child before marriage. When Jesse went to school, his classmates often teased him about being born out of **wedlock.** This hurt Jesse. He had to learn to put up with the teasing and succeed in spite of it.

Jesse always loved his mother. But his grandmother was the most important adult in his young life. She loved and raised him as if he were her own child. Matilda Burns worked as a maid for wealthy white families in Greenville. She cleaned and cooked so that Jesse could have opportunities she never had. She often brought home books and *National Geographic* magazines from her employers' homes. She wanted to give Jesse a look at the world outside Greenville. She encouraged him to do well in school.

The Burns family was very poor. They lived in a tiny, three-room house with a tin roof. The house was made of old wood and had no bathroom or running water. Sometimes, only the wallpaper kept the wind out of their home.

Courtesy of the Greenville Cultural Exchange Center

As a young boy, Jesse felt lonely and different from the other students at his school. But as he grew older, the support of his family helped him gain confidence and become a good student.

Just before Jesse turned two years old, his mother married a soldier named Charles Jackson. Soon, Jackson moved Jesse and his family into a nicer house. Jesse was happy to finally have solid brick walls and plumbing.

Today, Jesse Jackson can speak to poor people all over the world about **poverty.** He knows what it's like to be cold and not to have enough food to eat. Jesse Jackson tells poor people of every race not to let poverty steal their dreams.

When Jesse was growing up, African Americans and white people were **segregated** in the South. Whites in the government created laws that separated them from African Americans.

African American children and white children had to go to different schools. Whites and African Americans could not use the same city parks. If there was only one park, African Americans could not use it at all. Whites and African Americans were even forced to sit in different seats on buses. Whites sat in the front of the bus. African Americans sat in the back. African Americans were not allowed to have jobs that paid well or that gave them power. Whites kept these jobs for themselves. **Segregation laws** did not just separate African Americans and whites. They gave whites the best of everything.

Jesse hated these laws. When he was six years old, he went to a candy store with a friend. He was in a hurry and whistled at the white storeowner to serve them. The owner pulled a gun on Jesse in the middle of the store. He put the gun to Jesse's head and said, "You ever whistle at me again … I'll blow your head off!" The grown-up African Americans in the store did nothing to help little Jesse. They knew that they could get into trouble by standing up to a white man. Segregation laws always gave white people power over African Americans.

©Jacques M. Chenet/CORBIS

TODAY JESSE JACKSON IS ONE OF THE BEST KNOWN AND MOST RESPECTED BLACK LEADERS IN THE UNITED STATES, BUT HIS CHILDHOOD WAS NOT ALWAYS EASY.

BY THE TIME JESSE REACHED HIGH SCHOOL,
HE WAS A POPULAR LEADER AND A STAR
ATHLETE. OTHER STUDENTS ADMIRED HIS
FRIENDLY PERSONALITY AND HIS INTELLIGENCE.

Jesse learned to succeed in spite of white **racism.** With the help of his family, his teachers, and his church, he did very well in school from an early age. Many of his teachers remember him as a bright, hard-working student.

When Jesse was 15, his stepfather adopted him. Jesse Burns became Jesse Jackson. Jesse's talent and supportive family helped him have bigger dreams than many of his friends. He won a football **scholarship** to the University of Illinois at a time when few African Americans went to college at all. His community had high hopes for Jesse, and he lived up to them.

Jesse thought he would escape racism by leaving the South and attending the University of Illinois. He quickly discovered that racism was sometimes just as bad in the North as it was in the South. White students yelled racial comments at him, just as they had in Greenville. Jesse also faced **discrimination** on the football field. Jesse proved that he could escape the South, but he still could not escape racism.

Jesse left the University of Illinois after his first year there. He attended North Carolina Agricultural and Technical College in Greensboro instead. Most students at North Carolina A&T were African American. He felt much more at home in North Carolina than in Illinois. He quickly became a popular football star. He also met the woman he would later marry. Her name was Jacqueline Brown. Everybody called her Jackie. When Jesse first met Jackie, he said, "Girl, I'm going to marry you!" Jackie just laughed at him. But after they dated for a year, the young couple did get married.

Jackie and Jesse were college students in the early 1960s. At that time, the **Civil Rights Movement** was spreading to college campuses. In the late 1950s, African Americans had begun to **protest** against segregation and discrimination. These protesters wanted blacks to have the same legal rights as white people had.

JESSE'S SUCCESS WITH HIS HIGH SCHOOL FOOTBALL TEAM
(ABOVE) WON HIM A SCHOLARSHIP TO ATTEND THE UNIVERSITY
OF ILLINOIS. WHEN HE STARTED SCHOOL THERE, JESSE
LEARNED THAT RACISM EXISTED OUTSIDE THE SOUTH, TOO.

Some protesters began sitting in bus seats reserved for white people. Others sat at "Whites Only" lunch counters. Others marched in the streets to tell the world about the unfair laws. Many protesters were arrested or beaten. Some were killed. Some African Americans called the Civil Rights Movement the Black Freedom Movement.

Jesse avoided the Black Freedom Movement at first. He liked being popular. He also knew that his parents would not want him to risk his future by getting arrested. But when the protests finally came to his school, Jesse decided to get involved.

Many different groups protested racism and discrimination in the 1960s. Jesse joined a group called the Congress of Racial Equality (CORE). Jesse quickly became a leader of this group. Some members were happy that Jesse joined.

Other members thought he was more interested in getting attention than in ending racism. That view changed when the Greensboro police arrested Jesse after a protest march. They soon released him. But after his arrest, Jesse had won the respect of other protesters. They realized that he took the Civil Rights Movement very seriously.

Jesse was a protester, but he was also a college student who needed to graduate. What would he do after graduation? Jesse decided to attend a seminary, a school for people who want to become ministers.

Jesse wasn't sure he wanted to be a minister. But he knew he wanted to be a **reformer.** And the greatest reformer of that time was a minister named Martin Luther King, Jr. Jesse Jackson graduated from North Carolina A&T. He won a scholarship to attend Chicago Theological Seminary, a small school in Chicago, Illinois. Jesse was right back in the state he had left four years before.

Meeting a Hero

Jesse worked very hard to go to the seminary and raise a family at the same time. He took jobs and studied many hours each day. One evening in 1965, Jesse had a few spare minutes, so he turned on the television. He saw members of the Alabama State Police beating African American protesters. The protesters did not fight back. They did not believe in fighting violence with violence.

Many protestors during the Civil Rights Movement believed in **nonviolence.** In fact, it was the message that Martin Luther King taught. Jesse wasn't surprised that the protestors in Alabama didn't fight back. But he felt sick watching the police beat the protesters. Many of the protesters were older people. Others were children.

Jesse could barely sleep that night. The next day, he convinced a group of classmates and some of his teachers to go with him to Alabama. They went to help the protesters finish their march. Jesse and his companions drove all night to get there.

When they reached Alabama, they saw thousands of protestors. Many of them were African American, and many of them were white. A few were Native American. They had all come to help.

Martin Luther King and Jesse Jackson met in Alabama. King was Jesse's hero. It was not the very first time they had met. But it was the first time Jesse had really had a chance to talk to him.

©Bettmann/CORBIS

IN 1965, MARTIN LUTHER KING ORGANIZED PROTEST MARCHES IN SELMA, ALABAMA. HE HOPED TO DRAW ATTENTION TO DISCRIMINATION IN THAT CITY.

©Bettmann/CORBIS

THE PROTEST IN SELMA BECAME VIOLENT WHEN POLICE AND STATE TROOPERS
TRIED TO STOP IT. JESSE JACKSON WATCHED ON TELEVISION AS THE PEACEFUL
MARCH GREW VIOLENT. THE EVENT MADE HIM SO ANGRY THAT HE GATHERED A
GROUP OF FRIENDS. THEY TRAVELED TO SELMA AND JOINED THE PROTESTORS.

King and Jesse Jackson stayed in touch after that meeting. Soon, King asked Jesse to join the Southern Christian Leadership Conference (SCLC) staff. The SCLC was King's civil rights organization. King had a special project for Jesse.

Many racist businesses in Chicago would not hire African Americans. But these same companies sold their products to African Americans. Civil rights leaders fought this racism with a plan called "Operation Breadbasket." During this protest, the SCLC asked businesses to stop discriminating against African Americans. If they did not, African Americans would start a **boycott** against the company. They would stop buying whatever the company sold.

Operation Breadbasket worked! Many companies discovered that they lost too much money when African Americans stopped buying their goods. Some companies stopped discriminating against African Americans. Operation Breadbasket brought good jobs to many African Americans.

MARTIN LUTHER KING AND OTHER PROTEST LEADERS NOTICED JESSE'S CONFIDENCE AND LEADERSHIP SKILLS AT THE SELMA MARCH. JESSE'S HARD WORK IN ALABAMA HELPED THE MARCH CONTINUE. IT ALSO BROUGHT HIM CLOSER TO KING.

Otis L. Hairston, Jr.

Chicago Leader

Jesse Jackson gained a **reputation** as an excellent speaker and activist. At age 25, he thrilled the African American community with his fiery, poetic speech. They admired his sharp mind and his handsome looks.

On April 4, 1968, something terrible happened. Dr. Martin Luther King was assassinated in Memphis, Tennessee. Jesse was devastated. He lost a teacher, a brother, and a friend all at once. For a while, the Civil Rights Movement lost its strength. Everyone was grieving. The sorrow and uncertainty led to disagreements within the SCLC.

Jesse was the national director of Operation Breadbasket at the time. He had become well known across the country. Disagreements flared between Jesse and Ralph Abernathy, the new leader of the SCLC. Abernathy and other leaders thought Jesse simply wanted to get attention for himself. They did not trust Jesse to be a team player.

Three years later, Jesse left the SCLC. He started his own organization called Operation PUSH. PUSH stands for People United to Serve Humanity. Operation PUSH had many goals. The goals were similar to those of Operation Breadbasket. PUSH also worked to get more African Americans to vote. It encouraged African Americans to become more active in their children's educations, too.

PUSH had a few problems. Many people believed Jesse Jackson wasted money. A few people even believed he was not honest about how he spent the group's money. Some people who worked for him left PUSH. They felt he did not share enough responsibility.

©Flip Schulke/CORBIS

MARTIN LUTHER KING'S DEATH STUNNED THE LEADERS OF THE CIVIL RIGHTS MOVEMENT. WHEN JESSE (FAR RIGHT) ATTENDED KING'S FUNERAL, HE STOPPED TO COMFORT CORETTA SCOTT KING, THE WIDOW OF THE GREAT CIVIL RIGHTS LEADER.

©Jaques M. Chenet/CORBIS

LEADERS INCLUDING JESSE JACKSON (SECOND FROM LEFT) AND THE MAYOR OF ATLANTA (THIRD FROM LEFT) SAID A PRAYER TOGETHER AT AN OPERATION PUSH CONVENTION. ALTHOUGH PUSH HAS RUN INTO DIFFICULTIES, THE ORGANIZATION CONTINUES TO HELP AFRICAN AMERICANS TODAY.

Even with these problems, PUSH grew until Ronald Reagan became president of the United States in 1980. When President Reagan stopped giving government money to PUSH, the group struggled. Still, the group managed to survive. Even today, Jesse's organization works to help the African American community.

PUSH helped African Americans become leaders in their communities. Jesse gave powerful speeches and showed other African Americans how to fight for justice. They saw that they could change their lives and help other people. Jesse Jackson and PUSH helped people feel good about themselves. Jesse always ended PUSH meetings with this speech:

JESSE: I am—
AUDIENCE: *I am—*
JESSE: Somebody.
AUDIENCE: *Somebody.*
JESSE: I may be poor.
AUDIENCE: *I may be poor.*
JESSE: But I am—
AUDIENCE: *But I am—*
JESSE: Somebody.
AUDIENCE: *Somebody.*

JESSE: I may be uneducated.
AUDIENCE: *I may be uneducated.*
JESSE: But I am—
AUDIENCE: *But I am—*
JESSE: Somebody.
AUDIENCE: *Somebody.*
JESSE: I may be unskilled.
AUDIENCE: *I may be unskilled.*
JESSE: But I am—
AUDIENCE: *But I am—*
JESSE: Somebody.
AUDIENCE: *Somebody.*
JESSE: I may be on dope.
AUDIENCE: *I may be on dope.*
JESSE: I may have lost hope.
AUDIENCE: *I may have lost hope.*
JESSE: But I am somebody.
AUDIENCE: *But I am somebody.*
JESSE: I am — black — beautiful — proud — I must be respected — I must be protected!
AUDIENCE: *I am — black — beautiful — proud — I must be respected — I must be protected!*
JESSE: I am God's child!
AUDIENCE: *I am God's child!*
JESSE: What time is it?
AUDIENCE: *What time is it?*
JESSE: Nation time!
AUDIENCE: *Nation time!*
JESSE: All right—look out…

"Run, Jesse, Run!"

By 1983, most African Americans saw Jesse Jackson as the nation's most important black leader. In fact, Jesse was the only leader who could speak for most of the black community. Jesse began to see that he could speak for other people, too. He could speak for people in America who worked hard but didn't get paid much money. Many of these people felt that the new president, Ronald Reagan, had forgotten them.

Jesse's main goal in life was to help hardworking poor people. When Jesse thought about these people, he saw a "Rainbow **Coalition.**" This is the name Jesse gave to people of all races who had no voice in government and who wanted him to run for president. As the Rainbow Coalition grew, Jesse began to dream the impossible. He dreamed of being the first African American president.

Jesse held **rallies** in churches all across the South. At the rallies, crowds of people yelled, "Run, Jesse, run! Run, Jesse, run...." Jesse got the message. In November of 1983, he decided to try to run for president of the United States. He hoped the Democratic Party would **nominate** him as its candidate. But seven other men hoped to be nominated, too. He did not have as much money for his **campaign** as some of the other men did. But that did not stop him.

One month later, a U.S. Navy pilot named Robert Goodman was shot down in the Middle East. Goodman survived, but the government in the country of Syria put him in prison. Jesse had once met the president of Syria. He believed that he could get the African American pilot released if he traveled to that country.

©Lynn Goldsmith/CORBIS

THE RALLYING CRY DURING JESSE'S TWO PRESIDENTIAL CAMPAIGNS WAS "RUN, JESSE, RUN!" AFRICAN AMERICANS HOPED THERE WAS FINALLY A BLACK CANDIDATE WHO HAD A CHANCE TO WIN THE MOST IMPORTANT ELECTION IN THE COUNTRY.

JESSE JACKSON APPLAUDED FOR LIEUTENANT
ROBERT GOODMAN AT A LUNCH HELD IN THE
NAVY PILOT'S HONOR. JESSE HELPED GET
GOODMAN RELEASED FROM A SYRIAN PRISON.
MANY PEOPLE CLAIMED THAT JESSE TRAVELED
TO SYRIA NOT TO HELP GOODMAN, BUT TO
GET PUBLICITY FOR HIS CAMPAIGN.

The United States government did not want Jackson to go. Some people thought he would embarrass the government. Others believed he had too little information about the problem to go to Syria. Many reporters wrote that Jesse didn't want to help Goodman, he just wanted **publicity** for his election campaign. Jesse went to Syria anyway. He spoke to the Syrian president for a long time. The next day, the Syrian government released Robert Goodman. Jesse had won!

When Jesse returned home, many newspaper reporters attacked him. They said he should have stayed home. They said that he only went to draw attention to himself. Didn't the reporters see that Jesse brought the pilot home? These reporters hurt Jesse. They made him angry. Jesse told them he did what was right. Many Americans agreed with him. His trip to Syria did end up helping his campaign.

Jesse did well early in the race, even though his campaign had little money. But his campaign ran into trouble when he made a negative comment about Jewish people. Jesse made the comment in private, but reporters found out about it and told the public. Jesse denied making the comment at first. Later, he apologized for saying it.

Many people were angry about what Jesse said, even after he apologized. Some were angry that he lied about making the comment. Many people did not trust him anymore. His campaign never really recovered from his careless words.

Jesse's campaign suffered serious setbacks. But he surprised many people by doing well. He finished third out of seven candidates. Finally, the Democratic Party chose Walter Mondale as its candidate. Still, more people voted for Jesse than anyone had expected. Many of those votes came from white people who believed in Jesse and his message.

Jacques M. Chenet/CORBIS

JESSE JACKSON SAID HE WANTED TO HELP AMERICA'S POOR. HE ALSO
WANTED BETTER OPPORTUNITIES FOR PEOPLE IN LOW-PAYING JOBS. THIS
MESSAGE ATTRACTED AMERICANS — BOTH BLACK AND WHITE — TO
SUPPORT HIS PRESIDENTIAL CAMPAIGN.

The race for the Democratic nomination was over. Jesse was invited to give a speech at the party's convention. He spoke about how we need to work together in America:

America is not like a blanket — one piece of unbroken cloth, the same color, the same texture, the same size. America is more like a quilt — many patches, many pieces, many colors, many sizes, all woven and held together by a common thread.... All of us count and fit somewhere.

Jesse did not win the nomination, but he did inspire the nation. As he spoke, more and more people turned on their televisions to watch. By the end of the speech, 33 million people were watching. Some reporters said Jesse's speech was one of the best they had ever heard. Even people who did not like Jesse liked what he said.

Jesse showed millions of Americans that an African American could run for president. He gave African Americans hope that they could have a say in politics. He showed all Americans that they had things in common, regardless of race.

Some people believed Jesse would run for president again in 1988. They were right. This time, many more people thought he might win. Jesse was a **frontrunner** even before the election began. People knew him from the last election. They gave him more help this time.

Jesse also reached out to more people. His Rainbow Coalition grew bigger and bigger. Even some poor whites who were prejudiced against African Americans liked Jesse. Jesse spoke to them about being poor. He talked to them about not having jobs. They liked Jesse because he was on their side. Many people in the Rainbow Coalition surprised each other. They had things in common with lots of different people.

©Roger Ressmeyer/ORBIS

JESSE'S SUPPORTERS, CALLED THE "RAINBOW COALITION,"
HELD PHOTOS OF HIM AND WORE RAINBOW-COLORED SCARVES
AT THE DEMOCRATIC NATIONAL CONVENTION. EVEN THOUGH
SOME PEOPLE SAID NEGATIVE THINGS ABOUT JESSE, HIS
SUPPORTERS NEVER LOST THEIR FAITH IN HIM.

The 1988 election went better than the one before. For a few weeks, Jesse was even the number one candidate! He surprised the nation again and won millions of white people's votes. Even more African Americans voted for him this time. Jesse ran hard. But he finished in second place. Many people thought the winner should have chosen Jesse to be the candidate for vice president. But that did not happen.

For the second time, Jesse spoke on television from the Democratic National Convention. This time, the convention was held in Atlanta, Georgia. Jesse spoke on television again. Jesse spoke about the need for Americans to work together. He reminded everyone in the nation about their common ground.

Jesse did not become the president of the United States. But when he ran for president, he made a difference. He made the nation pay attention to poverty among people of all races. He encouraged millions of African American voters to cast their ballots for the first time. All these new voters elected governors, mayors, and members of Congress. These leaders cared about many of the same issues that the new voters did.

Jesse's biggest achievement was in the hearts and minds of Americans. In a 1983 **poll,** almost one in four Americans said they would not consider voting for an African American presidential candidate. That feeling has changed. In 1996, a retired African American army general named Colin Powell led in the polls — and he never even entered the race!

The Next Step

In August of 1990, Jesse traveled to the country of Iraq. The United States was about to go to war against that country. The Iraqi president, Saddam Hussein, held hundreds of foreigners, including Americans, as **hostages.**

Once again, Jesse traveled to a foreign country to talk with its leader. He did this to gain freedom for others. The U.S. government did not want Jesse to go to Iraq because the two nations were close to war. Jesse decided to go anyway.

Jesse convinced Saddam Hussein to release almost 300 people. But when he returned to the United States, reporters and the U.S. government treated him as though he did something wrong. Some people wondered who had paid for the trip. Others claimed it was just another publicity stunt. After his hard work, Jesse Jackson's own country refused to thank him for helping the hostages.

Jesse didn't give up, though. He has continued to travel to other countries. Sometimes he goes to help end **conflicts.** Other times, he goes to gain the release of hostages. No matter where he goes, people flock to meet him. They believe that he fights racism and helps poor people. Government officials greet him as an important visitor.

Some people thought Jesse would run for president again in 1992 and 1996. Jesse decided not to do it, saying he was too tired and that it put too much stress on his family. In 1995, he did help his son, Jesse Jr., win an election. That year, Jesse Jackson, Jr., was elected to the U.S. House of Representatives.

Jesse Sr. has never stopped working to help people, both in the United States and in other countries. He continues to help African Americans he believes have been treated unfairly. He speaks out against violence and drug use within the African American community. In 1997, he introduced an idea to improve educational opportunities for black children.

In 1999, Jesse traveled to Yugoslavia during the Kosovo War. He went to gain the release of three U.S. soldiers who were being held hostage. Shortly after his visit, the Yugoslav president freed the U.S. soldiers.

That same year, Jesse decided not to run for president in the 2000 election. His job, said Jackson, was not to run for president, but to help build a better country. No one knows for sure what Jesse Jackson's future holds. Whatever his next step, he will continue to show Americans, black and white, how to dream and how to achieve their goals.

©AFP/CORBIS

DURING THE KOSOVO WAR, THREE U.S. SOLDIERS WERE CAPTURED AND HELD IN PRISON. JESSE TRAVELED TO THE CAPITAL CITY OF YUGOSLAVIA TO HELP THE MEN. ON MAY 2, 1999, YUGOSLAVIAN LEADERS RELEASED THE SOLDIERS INTO JACKSON'S CUSTODY.

Timeline

1941	Jesse Louis Burns is born on October 8th.
1957	Jesse Burns takes his stepfather's name and becomes Jesse Louis Jackson on February 4th.
1959	Jackson graduates from Sterling High School in Greenville, South Carolina.
1959–1960	Jackson attends the University of Illinois.
1961	Jackson transfers to North Carolina Agricultural & Technical College.
1962	Jackson marries Jacqueline Lavinia Brown on December 31.
1963	Jackson becomes a leader of civil rights demonstrations in Greensboro, North Carolina. He is arrested for protesting.
1964	Jackson graduates from North Carolina A&T and enters the Chicago Theological Seminary.
1965	After watching an Alabama protest on television in which the protestors were violently beaten, Jackson is among thousands of people who head to Selma, Alabama. He meets Dr. Martin Luther King.
1966	Jackson becomes the head of the Chicago chapter of the Southern Christian Leadership Conference (SCLC) Operation Breadbasket.
1967	Jackson becomes the national director of Operation Breadbasket.

1968	Martin Luther King, Jr., is assassinated in Memphis, Tennessee, on April 4.
1971	After resigning from the SCLC, Jackson starts an organization called Operation PUSH.
1983	Jackson enters the 1984 Democratic presidential race. In December, he travels to Syria to help free U.S. pilot Robert Goodman.
1984	Jackson founds the National Rainbow Coalition. A negative comment Jackson makes about Jewish people hurts his election campaign.
1988	Jackson enters the presidential race for a second time. He eventually loses the nomination to Massachusetts Governor Michael Dukakis.
1990	Jackson wins the release of hundreds of hostages being held by the Iraqi president, Saddam Hussein.
1991	Jackson announces that he will not run for president in 1992.
1997	Jackson announces a plan to improve educational opportunities for black children.
1999	Jackson announces that he will not run for president in 2000. During the Kosovo war, Jackson goes to Belgrade, Yugoslavia, to seek the release of soldiers captured from a peace-keeping unit.

Glossary

activist (AK-tih-vist)
An activist is a person who speaks out and works for what he or she believes is right. Jesse Jackson is an activist.

boycott (BOY-kot)
A boycott is a form of protest in which people stop using a certain product or service. Boycotts were used frequently throughout the Civil Rights Movement.

campaign (kam-PAYN)
A campaign is a number of connected activities, such as giving speeches or traveling around the country to meet people, designed to help someone win an election. Jesse Jackson had little money to pay for his campaign.

candidate (KAN-dih-dayt)
A candidate is a person who seeks to be elected to a public office. Jesse Jackson was a presidential candidate in 1984 and 1988.

Civil Rights Movement (SIH-vel RYTZ MOOV-ment)
The Civil Rights Movement was the struggle for equal rights for African Americans in the United States during the 1950s and 1960s. Martin Luther King, Jr., was a leader of the Civil Rights Movement.

coalition (koh-uh-LIH-shun)
A coalition is a group of people who work together to get something done. The Rainbow Coalition is the name Jesse Jackson gave to people of all races who wanted him to be elected president.

conflicts (KON-flikts)
Conflicts are fights or struggles. Sometimes Jesse Jackson travels to foreign countries to help solve conflicts.

convention (kon-VEN-shun)
A convention is a meeting. The Democratic and Republican political parties hold conventions every four years to choose their presidential candidates.

demonstrations (deh-mun-STRAY-shunz)
Demonstrations are when groups of people with common goals or beliefs participate in a march, rally, or other public action to show their support for a cause.

discrimination (dis-krim-ih-NAY-shun)
Discrimination is the unfair treatment of people simply because they are different. African Americans have suffered discrimination by whites.

frontrunner (FRUNT-run-ur)
A frontrunner is a leader during an election campaign. Jesse Jackson was a frontrunner at the beginning of the 1988 presidential campaign.

hostages (HAW-steh-jez)
Hostages are people who are captured and held as prisoners until a demand is met. The Iraqi government held foreigners as hostages to try to keep the United States from declaring war.

justice (JUH-stiss)
Justice is fairness. Jesse Jackson led demonstrations for justice and equal rights.

nominate (NAW-meh-nayt)
To nominate someone is to choose them for public office. Jesse Jackson hoped members of the Democratic Party would nominate him as their candidate for president.

nonviolence (non-VY-uh-lentz)
Nonviolence is a way that people can demonstrate for change without hurting others. Civil rights workers were trained in nonviolence and learned not to respond with anger when anger was shown toward them.

political party (poh-LIH-tih-kull PAR-tee)
A political party is a group of people who share similar ideas about how to run a government. The Democrats and the Republicans are the two biggest political parties in the United States.

Glossary

politics (PAH-lih-tiks)
Politics refers to the actions and practices of the government. Most presidential candidates have had careers in politics or in the military.

poll (POHL)
A poll is a survey of people's opinions. In a 1983 poll, almost one in four Americans said they would not consider voting for an African American presidential candidate.

poverty (PAH-ver-tee)
Poverty is the condition of being poor. Jesse Jackson has focused attention on people who live in poverty.

prejudices (PREH-juh-dih-sez)
Prejudices are opinions about people or things that are made without careful thought or fairness. Jesse Jackson challenged many people to let go of their prejudices.

protest (PROH-test)
If people protest against something, they speak out to say that it is wrong. In the 1950s, African Americans began protesting against segregation and discrimination.

publicity (puh-BLIH-sih-tee)
Publicity is attention from the public. Some people claimed that Jesse Jackson helped U.S. Navy pilot Robert Goodman only to gain publicity.

racism (RAY-sih-zem)
Racism is a negative feeling or opinion about people because of their race. Racism can be committed by individuals, large groups, or even by governments.

rallies (RAL-eez)
Rallies are gatherings of people who come together to achieve a purpose. Jesse held rallies in churches all across the south.

reformer (ree-FOR-mur)
A reformer is someone who tries to change something for the better. Jesse Jackson is a reformer.

reputation (reh-pyoo-TAY-shun)
A reputation is what people say or think about another person. Jesse Jackson had a reputation as an excellent speaker and an activist.

scholarship (SKAHL-er-ship)
A scholarship is money awarded to a student to help pay for his or her education. Jesse Jackson received a scholarship to attend college.

segregated (SEH-grih-gay-ted)
If people are segregated, they are kept apart from others. For many years, African Americans in the South were segregated from white people.

segregation laws (seh-grih-GAY-shun LAWZ)
Segregation laws were laws that seperated white people from black people in the southern United States. Jesse Jackson grew up with segregation laws.

wedlock (WED-lok)
Wedlock is married life, or being married. Jesse Jackson was born out of wedlock, which means his parents were not married.

Index

Further Information

Books

Celsi, Teresa. *Jesse Jackson and Political Power (Gateway Civil Rights series)*. Brookfield, CT: Millbrook Press, 1994.

King, Casey. *Oh, Freedom: Kids Talk About the Civil Rights Movement*. Topeka, KS: Econo-Clad Books, 1999.

Levine, Ellen. *Freedom's Children: Young Civil Rights Activists Tell Their Own Stories*. New York: Avon, 1995.

Web Sites

Learn more about Jesse Jackson and listen to his speeches at the Democratic National Conventions:
http://www2.pbs.org/wgbh/pages/frontline/jesse/tindex.html

Visit the PUSH/Rainbow Coalition Web site:
http://www.rainbowpush.org

Visit the National Civil Rights Museum:
http://www.midsouth.rr.com/civilrights/